The Best
Dad
in the World

THIS IS A PRION BOOK

First published in Great Britain in 2016 by Prion
An imprint of the Carlton Publishing Group
20 Mortimer Street
London W1T 3JW

A CIP catalogue for this book is available from the British Library.

ISBN 978-1-85375-960-4

Printed in Dubai

10 9 8 7 6 5 4 3 2 1

The Best
Dad
in the World

Humorous and Inspirational Quotes
Celebrating Fantastic Fathers

PRION

Contents

Introduction

The greatest way to describe our dear old dads is to paraphrase the most poignant line from *Forrest Gump*: "Dads are like a box of chocolates, you never know what you're gonna get." Like the box of chocolates themselves, dads are indeed a nutty bunch. They can come in all shapes, sizes and packaging; some are squishy and some are tough, but we love them unconditionally.

No matter what they look like though, or how deliberately they try to embarrass us in front of our friends, dads are quite simply the best things since toast came buttered. From being the world's best shoulder to cry on to the cheapest late-night taxi service, not forgetting being the most accommodating hotel owner you'll ever meet, our poor put-upon fathers are there for us 24 hours a day, seven days a week – just like all good banks should be. Enjoy!

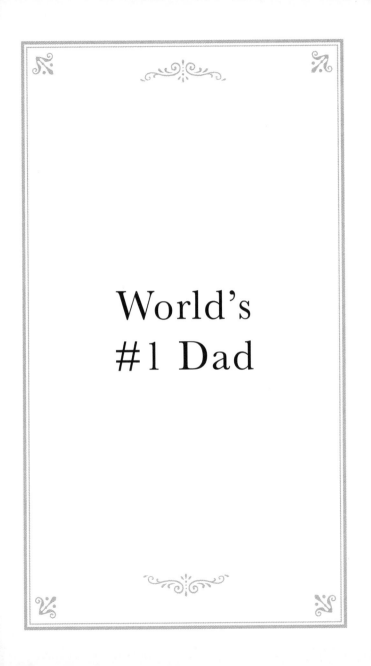

World's
#1 Dad

"I remember so clearly us going into hospital so Victoria could have Brooklyn. I was eating a Lion Bar at the time."

David Beckham

"Whenever one of my children says, 'Goodnight, Daddy,' I always think to myself, 'You don't mean that.'"

Jim Gaffigan

"When I was a kid, I said to my father one afternoon, 'Daddy, will you take me to the zoo?' He answered, 'If the zoo wants you, let them come and get you.'"

Jerry Lewis

"All my sons are named George Foreman. They all know where they came from."

George Foreman

"I think God made babies cute
so we don't eat them."

Robin Williams

"Somewhere on this globe, every
ten seconds, there is a woman
giving birth to a child. She must
be found and stopped."

Sam Levenson

"I don't have a kid, but I think that
I would be a good father, especially
if my baby liked to go out drinking."

Eugene Mirman

"My father had a profound
influence on me. He was a lunatic."

Spike Milligan

"I cannot understand how
I managed to cope without getting
cuddled this many times a day."

Russell Crowe

"If you have never been hated
by your child you have never
been a parent."

Bette Davis

"Noble fathers have noble children."

Euripides

"Every father should remember one day his son will follow his example, not his advice."

Charles Kettering

"Father! – to God himself we cannot give a holier name."

William Wordsworth

"I have a Father's Day every day."

Dennis Banks

"I killed the monsters.
That's what fathers do."

F. K. Wallace

"Why, 'tis a happy thing
To be the father unto many sons."

William Shakespeare

"I am not ashamed to say that no man I ever met was my father's equal, and I never loved any other man as much."

Hedy Lamarr

"Fathers should be neither seen nor heard. That is the only proper basis for family life."

Oscar Wilde

"I looked up to my dad.
He was always on a ladder."

David Chartrand

"My father wore the trousers
in the family – at least after
the court order."

Vernon Chapman

"I know one way guaranteed
to make my children scatter:
I get up and dance."

Terry Wogan

"I used to jog but the ice cubes kept
falling out of my glass."

Dave Lee Roth

"Well you're not gonna be picking a
fight, Dad... Dad... Daddy-o!"

Marty McFly, Back to the Future

"You will always be your child's
favourite toy."

Vicki Lansky

"You know how it is with fathers,
you never escape the idea that
maybe after all they're right."

John Updike

"The greatest mark of a father is
how he treats his children when
no one is looking."

Dan Pearce

"My father taught me to work, but not to love it. I never did like to work and I don't deny it. I'd rather read, tell stories, crack jokes, talk, laugh – anything but work."

Abraham Lincoln

"The older I get, the smarter my father seems to get."

Tim Russert

"Luke, I am your father."

Darth Vader, Star Wars

"The heart of a father is the masterpiece of nature."

Antoine François Prévost

"Dad always thought laughter was the best medicine, which I guess is why several of us died of tuberculosis."

Jack Handey

"A successful father is not more successful than his children."

Raheel Farooq

"By the time a man realizes
that maybe his father was right,
he usually has a son who thinks
he's wrong."

Charles Wadsworth

"One of the greatest titles in the
world is parent, and one of the
biggest blessings in the world is to
have parents to call mom and dad."

Jim DeMint

"Remember: what dad really
wants is a nap. Really."

Dave Barry

"Lately, all my friends are worried
that they're turning into their
fathers. I'm worried I'm not."

Dan Zevin

"I've done all kinds of cool things as an actor – I've jumped out of helicopters and done some daring stunts and played baseball in a professional stadium, but none of it means anything compared to being somebody's daddy."

Chris Pratt

"When one has not had a good father, one must create one."

Friedrich Nietzsche

"Don't eat me. I have a wife and kids. Eat them."

Homer Simpson

"My dad used to say 'Always fight fire with fire,' which is probably why he got thrown out of the the fire brigade."

Harry Hill

"Man, if I can get a burp out of that little thing I feel such a sense of accomplishment."

Brad Pitt

"My father gave me the greatest gift anyone could give another person: he believed in me."

Jim Valvano

"Having a kid is like falling in love for the first time when you're 12, but every day."

Mike Myers

"Any man can be a father, but it takes someone special to be a dad."

Anne Geddes

"I'm sure wherever my father is,
he's looking down on us. He's not
dead, just very condescending."

Jack Whitehall

"It is impossible to please all the
world and one's father."

Jean de La Fontaine

"The child is father of the man."

William Wordsworth

"A good husband makes a
good wife."

John Florio

"Watch your mouth, kid, or you'll
find yourself floating home."

Han Solo, Star Wars

"Every dad is entitled to one
hideous shirt and one horrible
sweater. It's part of the Dad Code."

Steve Martin

"If you can give your son or
daughter only one gift, let it
be enthusiasm."

Bruce Barton

"Holding these babies in my arms
makes me realize the miracle my
husband and I began."

Betty Ford

"Directly after God in heaven
comes Papa."

Wolfgang Amadeus Mozart

"Children make you want to
start life over."
Muhammad Ali

"The only thing worth stealing
is a kiss from a sleeping child."
Joe Houldsworth

"It is a wise father that knows
his own child."
William Shakespeare

Fatherhood
Rules

"Fatherhood is great because you can ruin someone from scratch."

Jon Stewart

"I won't lie to you, fatherhood isn't easy – like motherhood."

Homer Simpson

"The quickest way for a parent to get a child's attention is to sit down and look comfortable."

Lane Olinghouse

"I've been to war. I've raised twins.
If I had a choice, I'd rather
go to war."

George W. Bush

"There are three stages of a
man's life: he believes in Santa
Claus, he doesn't believe in
Santa Claus, he is Santa Claus."

Bob Philips

"Being a great father is like shaving. No matter how good you shaved today, you have to do it again tomorrow."

Reed Markham

"Who would be a father!"

William Shakespeare

"The secret of fatherhood is to know when to stop tickling."

Annie Pigeon

"I cannot think of any need in childhood as strong as the need for a father's protection."

Sigmund Freud

"A good father is a little bit of mother."

Lee Falk

"We all knew dad was the one in charge: he had control of the remote."

Raymond Bell

"Money isn't everything – but it sure keeps you in touch with your children."

John Paul Getty

"If you want to recapture your youth, cut off his allowance."

Al Bernstein

"The problem with the gene pool is that there is no lifeguard."

Steven Wright

"Children are nature's very own
form of birth control."

Dave Barry

"Don't worry – the first 40 years
are the worst."

Cliff Jackson

"Did you know babies are
nauseated by the smell
of a clean shirt?"

Jeff Foxworthy

"The worst feature of a new baby
is its mother's singing."

Kin Hubbard

"People who say they sleep like a
baby usually don't have one."

Leo J. Burke

"We learn from experience.
A man never wakes up his second
baby just to see it smile."

Grace Williams

"The beauty of 'spacing' children many years apart lies in the fact that parents have time to learn the mistakes that were made with the older ones – which permits them to make exactly the opposite mistakes with the younger ones."

Sydney J. Harris

"Your mother was a hamster and your father smelt of elderberries."

Monty Python and the Holy Grail

"I've got more paternity suits
than leisure suits."

Engelbert Humperdinck

"Children are the only form of
immortality that we can be sure of."

Peter Ustinov

"What's a home without
children? Quiet."

Henry Youngman

"Parenting, there's a tough job.
Easy to get though. I think most
people love the interview. You don't
even have to dress for it."

Steve Bruner

"I married your mother
because I wanted children.
Imagine my disappointment
when you came along."

Groucho Marx

"All babies are supposed to look like me – at both ends."

Winston Churchill

"I was so ugly at birth, the midwife took one look at me, turned and slapped my father."

Joan Rivers

"Thank goodness he hasn't got ears like his father!"

Queen Elizabeth II, on first seeing Prince William

"It is not flesh and blood
but the heart which makes
us fathers and sons."

Friedrich Schiller

"Yours is the Earth and
everything that's in it,
And – which is more –
you'll be a Man, my son!"

Rudyard Kipling

"My father worked for the same firm for 12 years. They fired him. They replaced him with a tiny gadget that does everything my father does, only it does it much better. The depressing thing is, my mother ran out and bought one."

Woody Allen

"My mother protected me from the world and my father threatened me with it."

Quentin Crisp

"Be a dad. Don't be 'mom's assistant'... Be a man... Fathers have skills that they never use at home. You run a landscaping business and you can't dress and feed a four-year-old? Take it on. Spend time with your kids... It won't take away your manhood, it will give it to you."

Louis C. K.

"When you have kids you do grow up. I have just started realising it now – it changes the world, having children."

David Beckham

"Fathers, like mothers, are not born. Men grow into fathers and fathering is a very important stage in their development."

David Gottesman

"My father probably thought the capital of the world was wherever he was at the time. It couldn't possibly be anyplace else. Where he and his wife were in their own home, that, for them, was the capital of the world."

Bob Dylan

"No word makes me happier
than the word 'daddy' uttered
by one of my children."

Michael Josephson

"I gave my father $100 and said, 'Buy
yourself something that will make
your life easier.' So he went out and
bought a present for my mother."

Rita Rudner

"Raising kids may be a thankless job
with ridiculous hours, but at least
the pay sucks."

Jim Gaffigan

"I never got along with my dad.
Kids used to come up to me and say,
'My dad can beat up your dad.'
I'd say, 'Yeah? When?'"

Bill Hicks

"I don't have a kid, but I think that I would be a good father, especially if my baby liked to go out drinking."

Eugene Mirman

"Becoming a father is easy enough, but being one can be very rough."

Wilhelm Busch

"The first half of our lives is ruined by our parents, the second half by our children."

Clarence Darrow

"She got her looks from her father.
He's a plastic surgeon."

Groucho Marx

"I am good, fun dad who teeters on
the edge of being embarrassing."

Barack Obama

"When a father gives to his son,
both laugh; when a son gives to his
father, both cry."

William Shakespeare

"Here's to alcohol: the source of, and
answer to, all of life's problems."

Homer Simpson

"Life was a lot simpler when what
we honoured was father and mother
rather than all major credit cards."

Robert Orben

"Dad taught me everything I know.
Unfortunately, he didn't teach me
everything he knows."

Al Unser, Jr.

"Having children is like having a bowling alley installed in your brain."

Martin Mull

"The surprising thing about fatherhood was finding my inner mush. Now I want to share it with the world."

Christopher Meloni

"The best way to make children good is to make them happy."

Oscar Wilde

"You don't really understand
human nature unless you know
why a child on a merry-go-round
will wave at his parents every time
around and why his parents will
always wave back."

William D. Tammeus

"A father is a man who expects
his son to be as good a man as
he meant to be."

Frank A. Clark

"If your kids are giving you a headache, follow the directions on the aspirin bottle, especially the part that says 'keep away from children.'"

Susan Savannah

"Make no mistake about why these babies are here; they are here to replace us."

Jerry Seinfeld

"To an adolescent, there is nothing
in the world more embarrassing
than a parent."

Dave Barry

"Money can't buy love, but it
improves your bargaining position."

Christopher Marlowe

"You can learn many things from
children. How much patience you
have, for instance."

Franklin P. Jones

"I guess I'm like any other concerned father, except that nobody else's son guns a cycle over 17 pickups without holding on to the handlebars."

Evel Knievel

"Have children while your parents are still young enough to take care of them."

Rita Rudner

"During the sole argument we had when Chelsea was in high school, I looked at her and said, 'As long as you're in this house, being president is my second most important job.'"

Bill Clinton

"Parents are the bone on which children sharpen their teeth."

Peter Ustinov

"Fatherhood? I love it. It introduced an element of fear into my life. When you're a bachelor, you don't give a shit. You can do anything. But when you become a father, you get scared about everything."

Alex Trebek

"My father was frightened of his mother. I was frightened of my father and I am damned well going to see to it that my children are frightened of me."

King George V

Sons and Daughters

"There are times when parenthood seems nothing more than feeding the hand that bites you."

Peter De Vries

"A two-year old is kind of like having a blender, but you don't have a top for it."

Jerry Seinfeld

"To a father growing old nothing is dearer than a daughter."

Euripides

"To be the father of growing daughters is to understand something of what Yeats evokes with his imperishable phrase 'terrible beauty'. Nothing can make one so happily exhilarated or so frightened: it's a solid lesson in the limitations of self to realize that your heart is running around inside someone else's body."

Christopher Hitchens

"A father is a man who prefers sleep over sex."

Ralph Anderson

"Watching your daughter being collected on a date is like handing over a $1 million dollar Stradivarius to a gorilla."

Jim Bishop

"What's weird is waking up every 45 minutes during the night and you're in a pleasant mood. Anything else that woke me up every 45 minutes in the middle of the night? You're dead!"

Ryan Reynolds

"Don't handicap your children by making their lives easy."

Robert A. Heinlein

"The problem with children is that you have to put up with their parents."

Charles DeLint

"Sing out loud in the car even, or especially, if it embarrasses your children."

Marilyn Penland

"If you want your children to improve, let them overhear the nice things you say about them to others."

Haim Ginott

"Teenagers complain there's nothing to do, then stay out all night doing it."

Bob Phillips

"If you would have a good wife, marry one who has been a good daughter."

Thomas Fuller

"A boy becomes an adult three
years before his parents think
he does, and about two years
after he thinks he does."

Lewis B. Hershey

"Many a man wishes he were
strong enough to tear a telephone
book in half, especially if he
has a teenage daughter."

Guy Lombardo

"You don't raise heroes, you raise sons. And if you treat them like sons, they'll turn out to be heroes, even if it's just in your own eyes."

Walter M. Schirra

"When I was a boy of 14, my father was so ignorant I could hardly stand to have the old man around. But when I got to be 21, I was astonished at how much he had learned in seven years."

Mark Twain

"It sometimes happens, even in the best of families, that a baby is born. This is not necessarily cause for alarm. The important thing is to keep your wits about you and borrow some money."

Elinor Goulding Smith

"A man knows he is growing old because he begins to look like his father."

Gabriel García Márquez

"Before I got married I had six theories about raising children; now I have six children and no theories."

John Wilmot

"Men should always change diapers. It's a very rewarding experience. It's mentally cleansing. It's like washing dishes, but imagine if the dishes were your kids, so you really love the dishes."

Chris Martin

"If I had a problem I could always call Daddy."

Martin Luther King, Jr.

"The sins of the father are to be laid upon the children."

William Shakespeare

"A good father is one of the most unsung, unpraised, unnoticed and yet one of the most valuable assets in our society."

Billy Graham

"Never raise your hand to your kids.
It leaves your groin unprotected."

Red Buttons

"The father of a daughter is
nothing but a high-class hostage."

Garrison Keillor

"When you're young, you think
your dad is Superman. Then you
grow up, and you realize he's just a
regular guy who wears a cape."

Dave Attell

"A truly rich man is one whose children run into his arms when his hands are empty."

Anon

"Anyone who tells you fatherhood is the greatest thing that can happen to you, they are understating it."

Mike Myers

"The father who does not teach his son his duties is equally guilty with the son who neglects them."

Confucius

"My daughter got me a
'World's Best Dad' mug.
So we know she's sarcastic."

Bob Odenkirk

"The best thing about being a dad?
Well, I think it's just the thing
that every man wants – to have
a son and heir."

George Best

"It behooves a father to be blameless
if he expects his child to be."

Homer

"My first outdoor cooking memories are full of erratic British summers, Dad swearing at a barbecue that he couldn't put together, and eventually eating charred sausages, feeling brilliant."

Jamie Oliver

"Every dad, if he takes time out of his busy life to reflect upon his fatherhood, can learn ways to become an even better dad."

Jack Baker

"Having a staring contest with a newborn is one of the weirdest things you'll ever do. And it is highly recommended."

Ross McCammon

"My wife is so analytical with raising kids and I am not. My feeling is if they turn out good, then that means I was a good daddy and put a lot of effort into it. If they turn out bad, it means they took after her side of the family."

Jeff Foxworthy

"The only Father's Day tradition in my family is the annual conversation he and I have where I say, 'Hey, Dad, what do you want for Father's Day this year?' and he says, 'Nothing.' Then I ask my mom what I should get him and she says, 'He likes sandalwood soap, dangly jewelry and Chanel No.5 perfume.'"

Michael Showalter

"Sons have always a rebellious wish to be disillusioned by that which charmed their fathers."

Aldous Huxley

"I've never protected the president, but I have been a new dad, and I can tell you that being a new dad is pretty terrifying. I'm pretty sure that something about the president makes the stakes a little higher, but to me as a new father, nothing is more important or scary than protecting a daughter."

Channing Tatum

"They don't grade fathers, but if your daughter is a stripper, you f---ed up."

Chris Rock

"Mother Nature is wonderful.
Children get too old for piggyback
rides just about the same time they
get too heavy for them."

Anon

"Children begin by loving their
parents; as they grow older they
judge them; sometimes they
forgive them."

Oscar Wilde

"There may be some doubt as to who are the best people to have charge of children, but there can be no doubt that parents are the worst."

George Bernard Shaw

"Nobody ever asks a father how he manages to combine marriage and a career."

Sam Ewing

"Kids, you tried your best
and you failed miserably.
The lesson is, never try."

Homer Simpson

"The greatest thing a father
can do for his daughter is
to love her mother."

Elaine S. Dalton

"Sometimes the poorest man leaves
his children the richest inheritance."

Ruth E. Renkel

"It is admirable for a man to take his son fishing, but there is a special place in heaven for the father who takes his daughter shopping."

John Sinor

"A father is always making his baby into a little woman. And when she is a woman he turns her back again."

Enid Bagnold

"Fathers are biological necessities, but social accidents."

Margaret Mead

"I want my son to wear a helmet 24 hours a day. If it was socially acceptable I'd be the first one to have my kid in a full helmet and like a cage across his face mask."

Will Arnett

"I love the comic opportunities that come up in the context of a father-son relationship."

Harrison Ford

"I found out that I'm a pretty bad father. I make a lot of mistakes and I don't know what I'm doing. But my kids love me. Go figure."

Louis C. K.

"The attitude you have as a parent is what your kids will learn from more than what you tell them. They don't remember what you try to teach them. They remember what you are."

Jim Henson

"One thing you can't do with babies, you can't give them steak."

Flavor Flav

"The guys who fear becoming fathers don't understand that fathering is not something perfect men do, but something that perfects the man. The end product of child-raising is not the child but the parent."

Frank Pittman

"The one thing children wear out faster than shoes is parents."

John J. Plomp

"His heritage to his children wasn't words or possessions, but an unspoken treasure, the treasure of his example as a man and father."

Will Rogers, Jr.

"Youth is a wonderful thing. What a crime to waste it on children."

George Bernard Shaw

"There are three ways to get something done: do it yourself, employ someone to do it or forbid your children from doing it."

Monta Crane

"Setting a good example for your children takes all the fun out of middle age."

William Feather

"Babies are such a nice way to start people."

Don Herold

"There really are places in the
heart you don't even know exist
until you love a child."

Anne Lamott

"Children are our second chance
to have a great parent-child
relationship."

Laura Schlessinger

"Don't try to make children grow up to be like you or they may do it."

Russell Baker

"It kills you to see them grow up. But I guess it would kill you quicker if they didn't."

Barbara Kingsolver

The Best
Advice for
Dads

"To be a successful father... there's one absolute rule: when you have a kid, don't look at it for the first two years."

Ernest Hemingway

"The trouble with being a parent is that by the time you are experienced, you are unemployed."

Anon

"Do not pray for an easy life, pray for the strength to endure a difficult one."

Bruce Lee

"Even very young children need to be informed about dying. Explain the concept of death very carefully to your child. This will make threatening him with it much more effective."

P. J. O'Rourke

"If your children spend most of their time in other people's houses, you're lucky; if they all congregate at your house, you're blessed."

Mignon McLaughlin

"What a child doesn't receive
he can seldom later give."

P. D. James

"Do what you can, with what
you have, where you are."

Theodore Roosevelt

"Rich men's sons are seldom
rich men's fathers."

Herbert Kaufman

"Labour doesn't end when the baby
is born; that's when it begins."

Anon

"The life of man is solitary, poor,
nasty, brutish and short."

Thomas Hobbes

"Beer makes you feel the way you
ought to feel without beer."

Henry Lawson

"I only know one thing and
that is I know nothing."

Socrates

"Don't argue with idiots because
they will drag you down to
their level and then beat you
with experience."

Greg King

"Never have children,
only grandchildren."

Gore Vidal

"The world is a dangerous place to live; not because of the people who are evil, but because of the people who don't do anything about it."

Albert Einstein

"Being a father is my most important role. If I fail at this, I fail at everything."

Mark Wahlberg

"I like work; it fascinates me. I can sit and look at it for hours."

Jerome K. Jerome

"When you have kids, there's no such thing as quality time. There's just time. There's no, 'Ooh, his graduation's better than going to the mall.' It's all kind of equal. Changing her diaper and her winning a contest – it's all good."

Chris Rock

"My dad always used to tell me that if they challenge you to an after-school fight, tell them you won't wait. You can kick their ass right now."

Cameron Diaz

"My father said there were two kinds of people in the world: givers and takers. The takers may eat better, but the givers sleep better."

Marlo Thomas

"I believe that what we become depends on what our fathers teach us at odd moments, when they aren't trying to teach us. We are formed by little scraps of wisdom."

Umberto Eco

"In my younger and more vulnerable years my father gave me some advice that I've been turning over in my mind ever since. 'Whenever you feel like criticising anyone,' he told me, 'just remember that all the people in this world haven't had the advantages that you've had.'"

F. Scott Fitzgerald

"If you're not failing every now and again, it's a sign you're not doing anything very innovative."

Woody Allen

"Do not spoil what you have
by desiring what you have not;
remember that what you now
have was once among the
things you only hoped for."

Epicurus

"Up until I became a father, it was
all about self-obsession. But then
I learned exactly what it's all about:
the delight of being a servant."

Eric Clapton

"Blessed indeed is the man who hears many gentle voices call him father."

Lydia M. Child

"Bart, a woman is like beer. They look good, they smell good, and you'd step over your own mother just to get one!"

Homer Simpson

"Let parents bequeath to their children not riches, but the spirit of reverence."

Plato

"I don't care how poor a man is;
if he has family, he's rich."

Dan Wilcox

"When my kids were younger,
I used to avoid them. I used to
sit on the toilet until my legs fell
asleep. You want to know why your
father spends so long on the toilet?
Because he's not sure he wants
to be a father."

Louis C. K.

"Four-year-old:
Tell me a scary story!
Me: One time little people popped
out of your mom, and they never
stopped asking questions.
Four-year-old: Why?"

James Breakwell

"Children are a great comfort in
your old age. And they help you
reach it faster too."

Lionel Kauffman

"Sometimes I am amazed that my wife and I created two human beings from scratch yet struggle to assemble the most basic of IKEA cabinets."

John Kinnear

"You don't have to deserve your mother's love. You have to deserve your father's. He's more particular."

Robert Frost

"My dad always had this little sign on his desk: 'The bigger your head is, the easier your shoes are to fill'. He really drilled that in."

Phil Jackson

"Having children is like living in a frat house – nobody sleeps, everything's broken and there's a lot of throwing up."

Ray Romano

"I have found the best way to give advice to your children is to find out what they want and then advise them to do it."

Harry S. Truman

"There should be a children's song: 'If you're happy and you know it, keep it to yourself and let your dad sleep.'"

Jim Gaffigan

"A father's disappointment can be
a very powerful tool."

Michael Bergin

"My father was not a failure. After
all, he was the father of a president
of the United States."

Harry S. Truman

"There must always be a struggle
between a father and son, while
one aims for power and the
other at independence."

Samuel Johnson

"It is much easier to become
a father than to be one."

Kent Nerburn

"The place of the father in the
modern suburban family is a
very small one, particularly
if he plays golf."

Bertrand Russell

"Laugh and the world laughs with
you, snore and you sleep alone."

Anthony Burgess

"My rule of life prescribed as an absolutely sacred rite smoking cigars and also the drinking of alcohol before, after and if need be during all meals and in the intervals between them."

Winston Churchill

"My goal is to hit the gym every day. Usually I just end up sleeping and drinking beer."

Gary Allan

"He was a wise man who
invented beer."

Plato

"Milk is for babies. When you
grow up you have to drink beer."

Arnold Schwarzenegger

"Men want the same thing from
their underwear that they want from
women: a little bit of support and
a little bit of freedom."

Jerry Seinfeld

"Education is not the filling of a
pail, but the lighting of a fire."

W. B. Yates

"A bath and a tenderloin steak.
Those are the high points of
a man's life."

Curt Siodmak

"Home is the place where,
when you have to go there,
they have to take you in."

Robert Frost

"Life is full of misery, loneliness, and suffering – and it's all over much too soon."

Woody Allen

"There is nothing like staying at home for real comfort."

Jane Austen

"Where parents do too much for their children, the children will not do much for themselves."

Elbert Hubbard

"The best thing to spend on
your children is your time."

Louise Hart

"When your child is talking,
turn off the world."

Crystal DeLarm Clymer

"There is too much fathering going
on just now and there is no doubt
about it, fathers are depressing."

Gertrude Stein

"I tell you, we are here on Earth to fart around, and don't let anybody tell you different."

Kurt Vonnegut

"I love deadlines. I love the whooshing noise they make as they go by."

Douglas Adams

"Love and fear. Everything the father of a family says must inspire one or the other."

Joseph Joubert

"Beer is living proof that God loves us and wants us to be happy."

Benjamin Franklin

"That is the thankless position of the father in the family – the provider for all and the enemy of all."

August Strindberg

"A baby is born with a need to be loved and never outgrows it."

Frank A. Clark

"A baby will make love stronger, days shorter, nights longer, bankroll smaller, home happier, clothes shabbier, the past forgotten and the future worth living for."

Carl Sandburg

"Drinking beer doesn't make you fat, it makes you lean... against bars, tables, chairs and poles."

Benjamin Franklin

"There are two lasting bequests we can give our children. One is roots. The other is wings."

Hodding Carter, Jr.

"I have reached an age when, if someone tells me to wear socks, I don't have to."

Albert Einstein

"If I had known how wonderful it would be to have grandchildren, I'd have had them first."

Lois Wyse

"It is easier to build strong children than to repair broken men."

Frederick Douglass

"Children have never been very good at listening to their elders, but they have never failed to imitate them."

James Baldwin

"Hard work is damn near as overrated as monogamy."

Huey P. Long

"I will always choose a lazy person to do a hard job, because a lazy person will find an easy way to do it."

Bill Gates

"The best way to appreciate your job is to imagine yourself without one."

Oscar Wilde

"I guess I don't so much mind being old, as I mind being fat and old."

Benjamin Franklin

"Until you have a son of your own...
you will never know the joy, the
love beyond feeling that resonates
in the heart of a father as he
looks upon his son."

Kent Nerburn

"Don't worry that children never
listen to you; worry that they are
always watching you."

Robert Fulghum

Married
With
Children

"Marriage is like a coffin and
each kid is another nail."

Homer Simpson

"Other things may change us,
but we start and end with family."

Anthony Brandt

"Behind every successful man
is a proud wife and a surprised
mother-in-law."

Hubert H. Humphrey

"Few things are more satisfying than seeing your children have teenagers of their own."

Doug Larson

"No man needs a vacation so much as the man who has just had one."

Elbert Hubbard

"The secrets of success are a good wife and a steady job. My wife told me."

Howard Nemerov

"Women will never be as successful as men because they have no wives to advise them."

Dick Van Dyke

"My advice to you is to get married: if you find a good wife you'll be happy; if not, you'll become a philosopher."

Socrates

"I'm so ugly my father carries around a picture of the kid who came with his wallet."

Rodney Dangerfield

"Having a baby changes the way you view your in-laws. I love it when they come to visit now. They can hold the baby and I can go out."

Matthew Broderick

"Give me the life of the boy whose mother is nurse, seamstress, washer-woman, cook, teacher, angel and saint, all in one, and whose father is guide, exemplar and friend.
No servants to come between.
These are the boys who are born to the best fortune."

Andrew Carnegie

"My father only hit me once –
but he used a Volvo."

Bob Monkhouse

"For rarely are sons similar to their
fathers; most are worse and a few
are better than their fathers."

Homer

"I love producing children. It's fun!
I don't like taking care of children,
but I love producing children."

Donald Trump

"A man's home is his wife's castle."

Alexander Chase

"You can tell what was the best year of your father's life, because they seem to freeze that clothing style and ride it out."

Jerry Seinfeld

"Humor is always based on a modicum of truth. Have you ever heard a joke about a father-in-law?"

Dick Clark

"Don't confuse Father's Day
with Valentine's Day, and here's
why. Boy, will you creep him out.
I can just tell you from last year,
uh, even if they do like chocolate,
they don't want it from their son."

Jon Stewart

"Undeservedly you will atone
for the sins of your fathers."

Horace

"Love begins by taking care of the closest ones – the ones at home."

Mother Teresa

"I've had bad luck with both my wives. The first one left me and the second one didn't."

Patrick Murray

"A man is only as faithful as his options."

Chris Rock

"God gave men a penis and a brain, but unfortunately not enough blood supply to run both at the same time."

Robin Williams

"My wife and I both made a list of five people we could sleep with. She read hers out: 'One, George Clooney; two, Brad Pitt; three, Justin Timberlake; four, Jake Gyllenhaal; five, Johnny Depp.' I thought, I've got the better deal here: 'One, your sister...'"

Michael McIntyre

"Wives are young men's mistresses, companions for middle age and old men's nurses."

Francis Bacon

"The calmest husbands make the stormiest wives."

Thomas Dekker

"Parenthood is the passing of a baton, followed by a lifelong disagreement as to who dropped it."

Robert Brault

"The child supplies the power, but the parents have to do the steering."

Benjamin Spock

"Husbands and wives generally understand when opposition will be vain."

Jane Austen

"Husbands are chiefly good as lovers when they are betraying their wives."

Marilyn Monroe

"Mother Nature, in her infinite wisdom, has instilled within each of us a powerful biological instinct to reproduce; this is her way of assuring that the human race, come what may, will never have any disposable income."

Dave Barry

"I said to the chemist, 'Can I have some sleeping pills for the wife?' He said, 'Why?' I said, 'She keeps waking up.'"

Les Dawson

"My wife is a sex object – every time I ask for sex, she objects."

Les Dawson

"Kids can be a pain in the neck when they're not a lump in your throat."

Barbara Johnson

"As a child my family's menu consisted of two choices: take it or leave it."

Buddy Hackett

"Humans are the only animals
that have children on purpose,
with the exception of guppies,
who like to eat theirs."

P. J. O'Rourke

"My friend has a baby. I'm
recording all the noises he makes so
later I can ask him what he meant."

Stephen Wright

"Every baby born into the world
is a finer one than the last."

Charles Dickens

"I once heard two ladies going on and on about the pains of childbirth and how men don't seem to know what real pain is. I asked if either of them ever got themselves caught in a zipper."

Emo Philips

"Age does not diminish the extreme disappointment of having a scoop of ice cream fall from the cone."

Jim Fiebig

"A father is a man who expects his children to be as good as he meant to be."

Carol Coats

"Giving birth is like taking your lower lip and forcing it over your head."

Carol Burnett

"Families with babies and families without are so sorry for each other."

Ed Howe

"The older I grow, the more
I distrust the familiar doctrine
that age brings wisdom."

H. L. Mencken

"Regrets are the natural
property of grey hairs."

Charles Dickens

"You know you've lived a few
years when you start having
your second thoughts first."

Robert Brault

"Men do not quit playing because they grow old; they grow old because they quit playing."

Oliver Wendell Holmes

"They told me that grandchildren are the reward you get for not killing your children."

Virginia Ironside

"My mother-in-law has so many wrinkles, when she smiles she looks like a Venetian blind."

Les Dawson

"My husband and I have never considered divorce... murder sometimes, but never divorce."

Joyce Brothers

"For a man wins nothing better than a good wife, and then again nothing deadlier than a bad one."

Hesiod

"A good marriage would be between
a blind wife and a deaf husband."

Michel de Montaigne

"Let the wife make the husband
glad to come home, and let him
make her sorry to see him leave."

Martin Luther

"The husband who decides to surprise his wife is often very much surprised himself."

Voltaire

"When I was young I thought that money was the most important thing in life; now that I am old I know that it is."

Oscar Wilde

"I believe that sex is one of the most beautiful, natural, wholesome things that money can buy."

Steve Martin

"I love the moments when I engage with my youngest daughter now. It's not my thing to sit on the ground and play tea party, but I'll do it because it's a moment that will stick with me forever."

Tim Allen

"When I come home, my daughter
will run to the door and give me
a big hug, and everything that's
happened that day just melts away."

Hugh Jackman

"Sometimes I wonder if men
and women really suit each other.
Perhaps they should live next door
and just visit now and then."

Katharine Hepburn

"You don't get older, you get better."

Shirley Bassey

"Love is something far more than desire for sexual intercourse; it is the principal means of escape from the loneliness which afflicts most men and women throughout the greater part of their lives."

Bertrand Russell

"Hate your job? Join our support group! It's called EVERYBODY. We meet at the bar."

Drew Carey

"A is success in life, then A is equal to X plus Y plus Z. Work is X; Y is play; and Z – keeping your mouth shut."

Albert Einstein

"There is no such thing as fun for the whole family."

Jerry Seinfeld

"I put my heart and my soul into my work, and have lost my mind in the process."

Vincent Van Gogh

"Before I met my husband,
I'd never fallen in love.
I'd stepped in it a few times."

Rita Rudner

"A friend never defends a husband
who gets his wife an electric skillet
for her birthday."

Erma Bombeck

"Nature gives us 12 years to
develop a love for our children
before turning them into teenagers."

William Galvin

"To show a child what has once delighted you, to find the child's delight added to your own, so that there is now a double delight seen in the glow of trust and affection, this is happiness."

J. B. Priestley

"Happiness is having a large, loving, caring, close-knit family in another city."

George Burns

"Rejoice with your family in
the beautiful land of life!"

Albert Einstein

"All women become like their
mothers. That is their tragedy.
No man does. That's his."

Oscar Wilde

"Before you marry a person, you
should first make them use a
computer with slow Internet to
see who they really are."

Will Ferrell

"There are only two ways to live your life. One is as though nothing is a miracle. The other is as though everything is a miracle."

Albert Einstein

"All happy families are alike; each unhappy family is unhappy in its own way."

Leo Tolstoy

"What's the point of children if you can't buy their love?"

Homer Simpson

"A great marriage is not when the 'perfect couple' comes together. It is when an imperfect couple learns to enjoy their differences."

Dave Meurer

"There is nothing nobler or more admirable than when two people who see eye to eye keep house as man and wife, confounding their enemies and delighting their friends."

Homer

"In my house I'm the boss, my wife is just the decision-maker."

Woody Allen

"The trouble with learning to parent on the job is that your child is the teacher."

Robert Brault

"Most of us become parents long before we have stopped being children."

Mignon McLaughlin

"My father didn't tell me how to live; he lived, and let me watch him do it."

Clarence B. Kelland

"When you become a parent, you begin to become sympathetic to your own parents. We begin to understand how much we owe to them, how much we're shaped by their vision of the world."

Philip Glass

"Having one child makes you a
parent; having two you are a referee."
David Frost

"Dining out with kids is brilliant.
They're the cheapest dates around.
They never order the lobster."
David Letterman

"All children alarm their parents,
if only because you are forever
expecting to encounter yourself."
Gore Vidal

"The fundamental defect of fathers
is that they want their children to
be a credit to them."

Bertrand Russell

"Regular naps prevent old
age, especially if you take
them while driving."

Anon

"Every man desires to live long,
but no man desires to be old."

Jonathan Swift

"Mothers are all slightly insane."

J. D. Salinger

"Your sons weren't made to like you. That's what grandchildren are for."

Jane Smiley

"Give me a woman who loves beer and I will conquer the world."

Kaiser Wilhelm